Quack Quack Duck

25 Delicious Duck Recipes

by
Pamela Shaw

Quack Quack Duck, 25 Delicious Duck Recipes

Version 2013.11.27

Print Edition 1.1

ISBN : 978-1494297725

Introduction

Quack Quack Duck is a compilation of some of the great duck dishes you can make a home for yourself, your friends and you family. It was not until I spent a family vacation in the famous Dordogne region of France that I became a passionate fan of duck.

The recipes in this book are divided into three sections; soups, salads and main dishes. Hence there are duck recipes for every season so you can always find a good excuse to prepare duck. The recipes include a mixture of Asian and European heritage.

There are some interesting health benefits to duck, which many people do not know. For example did you know the duck meat is good source of vitamin A, vitamin B3 and vitamin C, and also contains calcium, iron and selenium. But the truth is that duck has a fantastic flavor and not everybody has the recipes to enjoy it. Whether it is a spicy soup or a tangy main course you are looking for there is something to offer for everyone in this book.

I hope you enjoy these dishes as much as I have enjoyed them. There is a duck recipe for everyone and with luck you will find it in this book.

Sizing and Abbreviation

It makes sense that we just clarify the sizing and abbreviation used in this recipe book. Firstly, all of the recipes in this book are quoted first in imperial units with metric units in brackets.

Cup size can sometimes feel a bit ambiguous, so whenever a cup is referred to we are assuming a cup equals to 8 fluid ounces, which is approximately 227 ml.

A tablespoon, which has the abbreviation tbsp. in this book, is equal to half a fluid ounce, which equates to approximately 14 ml.

A teaspoon, which has the abbreviation tsp. in this book, is one sixth of a fluid ounce, which equates to approximately 5 ml.

All other abbreviations are standard, for example oz. for ounce, Kg for Kilogram.

Soups

Here we have five fantastic recipes for soups, each has a different flavor and all are worth the time to cook and enjoy. Perfect for the cold winter weather or a rainy Sunday afternoon.

Simple Duck Soup

This simple duck soup recipe makes a great winter warmer. It may be simple to make but don't let that fool you into thinking that it is not delicious. This makes a great starter or meal itself.

Ingredients for 4 good servings

- Salt, Pepper and Oregano. 6 oz. (170 g) Duck breast (1 duck breast).
- 8 oz. (225 g) Pak Choi (Chinese cabbage)
- 2 pints (950 ml) of duck or chicken stock
- 2 Garlic cloves
- 1 tbsp. rice wine
- 1 tbsp. soy sauce
- 1 tbsp. Sesame seeds
- 1 tsp. Sesame oil
- 1 Star Anise
- Fresh parsley

Preparation - 45 to 50 minutes

1. Remove the skin from the duck breast and finely dice the meat, discarding the skin.

2. Finely shred the Pak Choi (Chinese cabbage).

3. Peel and crush the garlic cloves.

4. In a large saucepan put the stock (duck or chicken), the soy sauce, the rice wine and the star anise.

5. Bring the saucepan to the boil and then add the cabbage, duck and the garlic. Stir it thoroughly.

6. Reduce the heat to maintain a simmer for 25 to 30 minutes.

7. When the duck meat is tender remove the star anise.

8. Chop the fresh parsley so that you have about 1 tbsp.

9. Add the sesame oil and the sesame seeds along with the freshly chopped parsley to the saucepan.

10. Stir through for several minutes and then serve in soup bowls.

11. Garnish with a little bit of freshly chopped parsley.

Goulash Duck Soup

A classic winter warmer, this goulash duck soup has ample vegetables and tender duck meat. Just an a great flavorsome soup that is a popular hit in any household.

A nice addition to this recipe to bulk it out and add some carbohydrates is to add some potato dumplings. These are not included in this recipe, but should you want to turn this soup into more of a meal give them a try.

Ingredients for 4 good servings

- 3 Duck leg joints

- 1¾ pints (900 ml) chicken stock

- 1 lb. (450 g) tomatoes

- 8 fl. oz. (228 ml) Dry White Wine

- 4 oz. (112 g) celeriac

- 4 oz. (112 g) fresh mushrooms

- 2 Onions

- 2 Garlic cloves

- 1 Red Pepper

- 1 Green Pepper

- 1 Large Carrot

- 6 tbsp. soured cream

- 2 tbsp. olive oil

- 2 tbsp. paprika

- 2 tbsp. plain flour

- 2 tbsp. parsley

- Half a tsp. caraway seeds

- 1 Bay leaf

- A pinch of Cayenne pepper

- Salt and Pepper

Preparation – 2 hours 15 minutes

1. In a large frying pan heat 1 tbsp. of olive oil over a medium to high heat.

2. Place the duck legs into the frying pan and brown on all sides.

3. Remove the duck legs from the pan and set aside to rest.

4. Add the wine to the same frying pan and boil until it is reduced to half. This will take about 5 minutes.

5. Remove the reduced wine from the heat and reserve.

6. Peel and chop up the onions and the garlic.

7. Deseed and dice both the red and green peppers.

8. Peel and dice both the carrot and the celeriac.

9. In a large saucepan heat 1 tbsp. of olive oil over a medium heat.

10. When hot add the garlic and onions and sauté for 5 minutes so that the onions become soft.

11. Now add the carrot, the celeriac and the peppers and cook for a further 5 minutes.

12. Add the caraway seeds and paprika and stir in thoroughly and cook for 2 minutes.

13. Add the flour to the saucepan and stir it in so that it coats the vegetables and cook for 3 minutes.

14. Rinse and slice the fresh mushrooms.

15. Rinse and dice the tomatoes.

16. Finely chop up the parsley so that you have 2 to 3 tbsp. full.

17. Add to the saucepan the chicken stock, the reserved wine, the mushrooms, the tomatoes, the bay leaf, the chopped parsley and the cayenne pepper and stir thoroughly.

18. Add the duck legs to the saucepan and bring it to the boil.

19. When boiling, reduce to a simmer, cover the saucepan and leave simmer for 1 hour so that the duck meat becomes tender.

20. Now that the duck meat is tender remove the legs from the saucepan. Shred the meat from the duck legs and return the meat to the saucepan.

21. Serve the soup in bowls.

22. To garnish the soup in the bowl add a dollop of soured cream and a sprinkle of freshly chopped parsley.

White Bean with Duck Confit Soup

Similar to duck cassoulet, the succulent flavor of the duck confit is present in every spoon full. This is another winter classic, which has plenty of vegetables to enjoy. Note that for the best results you will need to soak the beans overnight.

Ingredients for 6 good servings

- 4 Confit Duck legs

- 1 lb. (450 g) dried cannellini (white beans)

- 1 can (14 oz.) of diced tomatoes.

- 2 Carrots

- 2 Celery sticks

- 2 Onions

- 4 Garlic cloves

- 8 cups water

- 5 cups chicken broth

- 3 tbsp. olive oil

- 2 whole cloves

- 2 large thyme sprigs

- 2 Bay leaves

- Half cup Cognac (Armagnac if possible)

Preparation - 11 hour hours 30 minutes (overnight)

1. The night before you will need to put the beans in a large pot of cold water. The water should cover the beans by a good 2 inches (5 cm). Leave the lid on the pot overnight for at least 10 hours.

2. Remove the meat from the duck legs, putting both the skins and bones to one side.

3. Coarsely shred the duck meat.

4. Peel and finely chop up the carrots, the garlic cloves and the onions.

5. Rinse and finely chop up the celery sticks.

6. Put the olive oil in a large pot over a medium heat.

7. When the oil is hot, cook the duck bones, the carrots, the garlic, the celery, the onions, the bay leaves, the cloves and the thyme. Stir occasionally and cook for 8 to 10 minutes until all the vegetables are soft.

8. Drain the can of diced tomatoes.

9. Drain the soaked beans and add them to the pot

along with the diced tomatoes, the water and the broth and then partially cover the pot with the lid.

10. Adjust the heat to maintain a simmer for 50 minutes. During this time stir and skim any scum from the surface.

11. While the pot is simmering thinly slice the reserved duck skin and season with a pinch of salt and pepper.

12. Cook the duck skin in a non-stick frying pan over a low heat until the skin is crispy and the fat is rendered. This will take about 8 to 10 minutes.

13. Remove and discard the bones, thyme and bay leaves from the pot.

14. Transfer 1 cup of liquid and 2 cups solid from the pot to a food processor and blitz until the liquid is smooth. Then return it to the pot with the rest of the soup.

15. Add 1 tsp. of salt and 1 tsp. of pepper to the pot and stir it in.

16. In a small saucepan over a low heat place the half cup of Cognac (Armagnac if possible) and with caution light it with a match.

17. When the flame has gone out, add the cognac to the soup and stir it in.

18. Serve the soup in bowls and garnish with the crispy duck skin.

Peking Duck Noodle Soup

This is a classic Asian duck noodle soup, which has a good balance of spices that will appeal to almost every pallet.

You can adjust the spiciness with the hot spicy sauce. Try to find Sriracha sauce if possible, which is actually a sauce from Thailand. You should be able to find it in an Asian supermarket.

Ingredients for 4 good servings

Broth:

- Bones from 1 duck

- 2 Carrots

- 2 Celery stalks

- 1 Onion

- 1 Garlic clove

- 2 inches (5 cm) fresh ginger

- 2 Lime leaves

- 3 tbsp. Vegetable oil

- 2 tsp. Black peppercorns

- Salt and pepper

Soup:

- 2 Duck breasts – cooked
- 1 packet of wonton egg noodles
- 2 Baby Bok Choy (Chinese Cabbage)
- 1 Fist full of scallions
- 1 Lime
- 1 Hot red chili
- 1 tbsp. Soy sauce
- Handful of basil leaves
- Hot Spicy Sauce (Sriracha if possible).

Preparation – 4 hours

Broth:

1. Heat the oil in a very large pot over a medium to high heat.

2. Break up the bones from the duck and sear them on all sides so that they are golden brown. This will take about 5 minutes.

3. Peel and chop the carrots and the onion.

4. Rinse and chop up the scallions and the celery stalks.

5. Peel and mince the garlic clove.

6. Thinly slice the piece of fresh ginger.

7.   Add the carrots, onion, scallions, celery, garlic and ginger to the pot and cook for another 5 minutes so that they have caramelized.

8.   Add the black peppercorns, the 2 lime leaves and season with salt and pepper along with adding 8 pints (3.8 l) of water to the pot.

9.   Reduce the heat to a simmer and leave for 3 hours.

10. Remove the pot from the heat and leave to rest for 20 minutes.

11. Sieve through the broth to remove the fat and return the broth to the large pot.

Soup:

12. Rinse and chop up the Bok Choy and the scallions.

13. Cut the red chili into thin strips. You can deseed if you want to avoid the kick, or leave the seeds in depending on you taste.

14. Add all of the vegetables from the soup ingredients list along with the soy sauce to the pot with the broth in it.

15. Place the pot over a medium to high heat and simmer for 5 minutes.

16. While the pot is simmering cook the egg noodles per the instructions on the packet. This will typically only take only a few minutes.

17. Diagonally thinly slice the cooked duck breasts.

18. In serving bowls first place the noodles

followed by the duck slices and pour the soup from the pot over the top making sure to include some vegetables in each bowl.

19.   Garnish each bowl with some basil leaves, a slice and lime (cut the lime into quarters) and for an added kick you can also add some spicy sauce.

Duck Soup with Rice and Sweet Potatoes

This is a very tasty soup with a savory broth. The rice and sweet potatoes add both substance and contrast to the soup. This one will quickly become a family favorite.

Ingredients for 4 good servings

- 1 Whole Duck (4 - 5 lbs)

- 28 oz. (830 ml) Beef broth (2 x 14 oz. cans)

- 28 oz. (830 ml) Chicken broth (2 x 14 oz. cans)

- 12 oz. (340 g) Sweet potato

- 2 Carrots

- 2 Celery stalks

- 4 cups of water

- 1 Large onion

- 1 Cup of long grain brown rice

- 1 Cup frozen tiny peas

- 2 tsp. ground cumin

- 1 tsp. powdered ginger

- 1 tsp. dried thyme

- 10 fresh sage leaves

- 1 Bay Leaf

Preparation – 2 hours 15 minutes

1. Remove the skin from the duck.

2. Lightly grease the bottom of a large saucepan with the skin from the duck.

3. Place the saucepan over a medium heat.

4. Chop up the duck into pieces.

5. Add the chopped up duck pieces to the saucepan and brown them.

6. Add the 4 cups of water 2 cans of chicken broth and 2 cans of beef broth to the saucepan.

7. Bring the saucepan to the boil. Skim away any fat or scum that forms.

8. Peel and roughly chop the carrots and the onion.

9. Rinse and roughly chop the celery.

10. Chop of the fresh sage until you have 1 tbsp. full.

11. Add the carrots, onion, celery, bay leaf, ginger, cumin, thyme and sage leaves to the saucepan.

12. Bring the saucepan back to the boil then reduce to a simmer for 50 minutes.

13. Remove the pieces of duck from the saucepan and put aside to cool.

14. Sieve and degrease the stock and then return it to the saucepan.

15. Add the rice to the saucepan and bring to the

boil then simmer for 20 to 25 minutes.

16.   While the rice is cooking remove the duck meat from the bones and dice it into thumb size pieces.

17.   Peel and dice the sweet potatoes (or yams).

18.   When the rice is cooked add the sweet potatoes and duck meat back to the saucepan.

19.   Bring the saucepan to the boil and then reduce the heat and simmer for 20 minutes.

20.   Add the handful of frozen peas to the saucepan and simmer for 5 minutes so that they are soft.

21.   Serve in soup bowls and add some freshly chopped sage as garnish.

Salads

Here we have a selection of five fantastic duck salads. These are all great salads for the spring and summer and provide us some tasty alternatives when preparing salad for family and friends.

Mango Duck Salad

What could make a more refreshing salad than mango and duck? The sweetness of the mango makes the perfect contrast for the duck. This is great a spring or summer salad.

Ingredients for 4 servings

- 2 lbs. (900 g) of roasted duck (half a duck)
- 4 oz. (115)g baby spinach leaves or mixed salad leaves
- 2 oz. (55 g) snow peas
- 2 ripe Avocados
- 1 ripe Mango
- 1 Spring onion
- Half a red pepper
- Qtr. of a cup mint leaves

Ginger Sesame Dressing:

- 2 tsp. Fish sauce

- 1 tsp. Grated fresh ginger

- 1 tsp. Soft brown sugar

- 1 tbsp. Soy sauce

- 1 tsp. Sesame oil

- 1 tbsp. Rice vinegar

- 1 small Red chili

- Qtr. cup lime or lemon juice

- Salt and ground black pepper

Preparation – 20 to 30 minutes

1. Deseed and finely chop the small red chili.

2. Using a sealable container (an old jam jar with its lid works pretty well for this) shake the sesame oil, lime juice, brown sugar, chili, soy sauce ginger, rice vinegar, salt and pepper together. (Note that you can keep this dressing in the fridge for several days, a week maximum.)

3. Strip the cooked duck from the bones and discard the skin and the fat.

4. Place the stripped duck meat in a bowl with half of the dressing and toss the dressing over the duck meat to coat it.

5. Boil some water and then pour this over the snow peas. Use a kettle for this as it is quicker and you don't need much water.

6.   Immediately drain the snow peas and then cover with cold water and drain.

7.   Peel both the mango and avocados. Remove the stones and then chop them up.

8.   Finely slice the small red pepper, the spring onion and the mint leaves.

9.   Rinse the spinach leaves and place them on a plate. Then add the snow peas, avocado, red pepper, mango, spring onion and the chopped mint.

10.   Place the strips of duck on top along with the remaining dressing and toss prior to serving.

Asian Duck Salad

The crunchy bean sprouts with the tasty duck make this a classic Asian salad. This is a very easy salad to prepare and not only is it delicious it is fresh and healthy.

Ingredients for 4 servings

- 2 or 3 Large Duck Breasts 1 lb. (450g)
- 8 oz. (227 g) Bok Choy (Chinese cabbage)
- 4 oz. (110 g) Sugar snap peas
- 4 oz. (110 g) Snow peas
- 4 oz. (110 g) Bean sprouts
- 1 Carrot
- 2 Green Shallots
- 1 Red Chili
- 1 oz. (30 g) Flaked almonds
- 1 firmly packed cup of coriander leaves
- Coriander sprigs.

Dressing

- 2 Limes

- 2 Garlic cloves

- 1 tbsp. Tamari sauce

- 1 tsp. Sesame Oil

- 1 small piece of fresh Ginger

- Qtr. tsp. Honey

Preparation - 30 minutes

Dressing

1. Finely grate the ginger until you have 1 tsp. full.

2. Squeeze the 2 limes. This should yield approximately quarter of a cup.

3. Peel and finely chop the garlic cloves.

4. In bowl combine the lime juice, the finely chopped garlic, the grated ginger the honey, the tamari sauce and the sesame oil.

The Duck

5. Heat a non-stick frying pan over a medium heat.

6. Remove the skin from the duck breasts.

7. Cook the duck breasts for 4 minutes on each side in the frying pan. You may want to cook a little less or a little more depending on how you like you duck to be served.

8. When cooked on both sides remove the duck breasts from the frying pan and cover with foil

on a plate for at least 10 to 15 minutes.

9.	While the duck is resting finely shred the Bok Choy (Chinese cabbage).

10.	Trim the sugar snap peas, and trim the ends of the bean sprouts.

11.	Trim the snow peas and then slice thinly lengthways.

12.	Peel the carrot and cut it into thin batons.

13.	Trim the ends of the shallots and then halve them and thinly slice lengthways.

14.	Deseed the chili and then thinly slice lengthways.

15.	Boil some water in the kettle.

16.	Combine the sugar snap peas, the carrot, the snow peas and the chili in a heatproof bowl. Then cover with the boiling water.

17.	Drain the hot water immediately and refresh the bowl under cold water.

18.	Thinly slice the duck breasts across the grain.

19.	Add the thin slices of duck meat to the mixture (from step 16) along with the bean sprouts, the shredded cabbage, the shallots, the almonds and the coriander.

20.	Drizzle half of the dressing over the bowl and toss thoroughly to combine.

21.	Serve the salad on 4 plates and drizzle the remaining dressing equally between the plates.

22. As a final touch sprinkle the plates with the coriander sprigs and serve.

Duck Confit and Pear Salad

What could be more classic French than pears with Roquefort? This salad is a real gem and will be sure to impress your family and friends.

Ingredients for 4 servings

- 2 Confit Duck legs
- 3 Pears (firm and ripe, Anjou if possible)
- 8 cups of mixed greens (baby spinach, watercress, endive)
- Half a cup of pecans
- 2 oz. (55 g) of Roquefort cheese - crumbled.
- 6 tbsp. Virgin olive oil
- 1 Shallot
- 1 tbsp. of Sherry vinegar
- 1 tsp. Dijon mustard

Preparation - 1 hour

1. Preheat the oven to 250°F (120 C).

2. Finely chop the shallot.

3. Put the sherry vinegar and Dijon mustard in a bowl along with a pinch of salt and pepper and

whisk.

4.   Pour 5 tbsp. of virgin oil into the mixture and whisk continually.

5.   Add the chopped shallot and whisk it in also.

6.   Put the remaining 1 tbsp. of olive oil in a heavy skillet and place over a medium heat.

7.   Coarsely chop the half cup of pecans.

8.   When the oil in the skillet is hot cook the pecans until golden brown. Remember to stir them whilst cooking.

9.   Remove the cooked pecans from the skillet and drain in paper towels. Season the pecans with a couple of pinches of salt.

10.   Increase the heat to high and place the skillet over it.

11.   Place the confit duck legs in the skillet skin side down and cook on all sides until the duck is crisp on all sides. This will take 5 to 10 minutes.

12.   Remove the duck from the skillet and tear the meat up into bite size pieces discarding the bones.

13.   Cover the pieces of duck with foil and keep warm.

14.   Halve and core the 3 pears and then cut them lengthways into slices.

15.   In a large bowl add the duck, pears, the mixed greens, the pecans, the dressing and crumble in the Roquefort cheese.

16.   Toss the contents of the bowl and then serve.

BBQ Duck and Noodle Salad

The fresh mint and coriander combine delightfully with the richness of the duck. You can either purchase a roast duck from your local Chinese supermarket or follow the recipe for Peking Duck in this book to prepare your own. The preparation time assumes that you purchasing a roast duck.

Ingredients for 4 servings

- 14 oz. (400 g) Egg noodles
- 1 Roast Duck (Chinese) - either purchase or see the Peking duck recipe in this book.
- 3 spring onions
- 2 Lebanese cucumbers
- 1 cup of snow pea shoots
- Half a cup of Coriander leaves
- Half a cup of Mint leaves

Dressing:

- 2 Limes
- 1 Red Chili
- Half a cup of Soy sauce
- 2 tbsp. Balsamic vinegar

- 2 tbsp. Sugar

- 2 tsp. of Sesame Oil

Preparation – 20 minutes

1. Boil water in a large saucepan and cook the noodles according to the instructions on the packet.

2. Whilst the noodles are cooking finely slice the spring onions and slice the cucumbers diagonally in half.

3. Also, blanch the snow pea shoots - put them in a pan of boiling water for 1 minute then remove and run under cold water.

4. Diagonally slice the snow pea shoots.

5. When the noodles are cooked rinse them with cold water.

6. Using your fingers pull the meat and skin from the cold (or slightly warm if you prefer, but not hot) duck. Shred the skin.

7. Put the noodles into 4 serving bowls along with the duck, coriander, mint and cucumber. Toss these together.

8. For the dressing finely slice the red chili pepper.

9. Freshly squeeze limes until you have quarter or a cup.

10. In a separate bowl combine the sliced red chili, the lime juice, the sugar, the balsamic vinegar

and the soy sauce. Stir together thoroughly.

11.   Drizzle the dressing over the bowls of noodle
        and serve with the spring onions.

Duck, Watermelon & Herd Salad with Cashews

The herd salad and watermelon provide a sour element, which combines beautifully with the rich flavor of the duck in this recipe.

Ingredients for 4 Servings

- 4 Duck breasts, skin on

- 2 Romaine lettuces

- 1 lb. (450 g) Watermelon

- 6 oz. (150 g) Radishes

- 4 oz. (115 g) Roasted cashews

- 3 Spring onions

- 2 Pink grapefruits

- 1 handful of mint leaves

- 1 handful of basil leaves

- 1 handful of coriander leaves

Dressing:

- 1 Red chili

- 1 Green chili

- 2 tbsp. Palm sugar

- 2 tbsp. Lime juice

- 2 tbsp. Fish sauce

- 1 tbsp. Tamarind paste

Preparation – 50 to 60 minutes

1. Score the skin of the ducks all the way through but make sure not to score or cut the meat of the duck.

2. Generously season the duck skin with salt and freshly ground black pepper.

3. Put the seasoned duck breasts skin side down in a large frying pan. (You may need to repeat steps 3 to 7 depending on the size of your pan and the duck breasts so that you can cook all of them.)

4. Put the pan over a medium heat and leave for 10 to 12 minutes.

5. The skin should now be brown and crispy and most of the fat will have melted into the pan. Spoon out the excess fat and season the topside of the duck.

6. Turn the duck breasts over and cook for 2 minutes.

7. Raise the temperature to high and cook for 1 minute before removing the duck breasts from the heat and leaving them in the pan to rest for

5 minutes.

8.   Deseed the chili's and then chop them up.

9.   Put the chili's, the palm sugar, the lime juice, the
      fish sauce and the tamarind paste into a food
      processor and blitz.

10.   Discard the outer leaves of the lettuce and peel
      away the inner leaves and place them on a large
      serving plate.

11.   Cut the watermelon into 1 inch chunks.

12.   Wash and thinly slice the radishes.

13.   Wash and cut the spring onions lengthways.

14.   Segment the grapefruit.

15.   Roughly chop the roasted cashew nuts.

16.   Thinly slice the duck breasts.

17.   Combine and toss the thinly sliced duck with
      the watermelon, grapefruit, radishes, the herbs
      and about half of the dressing.

18.   Spread this out over the lettuce leaves on the
      serving plate.

19.   Top with the roughly chopped cashews
      followed by the remaining half of the dressing.

20.   Serve and enjoy.

Main Dishes

Here we have a selection of main dishes from Asia that include curries and fried rice, some French recipes including a fantastic duck cassoulet and a tasty tagliatelle pasta.

Duck Confit with French Dressing

This is a French classic. You will be sure to impressive family and friends with this delicious recipe.

Ingredients for 4 servings

- 4 Confit Duck legs – with skin

- 2 lbs. (1 kg) Potatoes, (ideally desiree)

- 4 Shallots

- 1 cup (250ml) White wine

- 1 cup (250ml) Chicken stock

- 1 tbsp. Dijon mustard

- 1 tbsp. each finely chopped flat-leaf parsley and tarragon leaves (see note)

- 6 Tomatoes

- 14 oz. (400 g) baby green beans

Preparation – 1 hour 20 minutes

1) Preheat the oven to 390°F (200°C).

2) Whilst the oven is preheating: Peel and chop the potatoes into pieces of approximately 1 inch (2

cm).

3)   Finely chop the shallots.

4)   Add the chopped potatoes to a large pan of lightly salted water and bring to the boil. Cook for 8-10 minutes until the potatoes are almost tender. Then drain the potatoes.

5)   Line a baking tray with baking paper.

6)   Carefully scrape off the excess fat from duck and set aside (see step 9). Place 2 tbsp. of this duck fat in a baking tray and put in the oven for 2-3 minutes until is melts.

7)   Now toss the potatoes in the fat and season them with salt and pepper. Roast the potatoes for 10 minutes on the baking tray.

8)   Place the duck on the lined tray and roast together with the potatoes for a further 20 minutes. Turn the potatoes once, and continue to roast until both the duck and potatoes are golden and crispy.

9)   Heat 1 tbsp. of the reserved duck fat (from step 6) in a pan over a medium heat.

10)   Cook the finely chopped shallot, stirring for 1-2 minutes until soft.

11)   Add the white wine and increase the heat from medium to high. Simmer this for 8-10 minutes until it is reduced to approximately 2 tbsp.

12)   Add the chicken stock and simmer for 6-8 minutes until the mixture is reduced half.

13) Now whisk in the mustard and herbs to this mixture to make the dressing.

14) Quarter the tomatoes, remove then seeds and then cut them up into strips.

15) Boil enough water to blanch the beans and then refresh them under cold water.

16) Toss the tomatoes together with the beans and half the dressing.

17) Serve the duck sat on the potatoes and tomato/bean mixture and drizzle on the other half of the dressing.

Fragrant Thai Duck Curry

This is a fantastic aromatic Thai curry recipe that really works well with the richness of the duck.

Note that the rice needed is not included as part of this recipe and you should allow yourself 20 minutes to cook it. The most suitable rice is Thai Jasmine rice.

Ingredients for 4 servings

- 4 Duck Breasts
- 28 oz. (830ml) Coconut milk (2 x 14 oz. cans)
- 3 Garlic gloves
- 3 Shallots
- 2 Red chilies
- 2 tbsp. olive oil
- 1 inch (2.5 cm) piece fresh ginger
- 4 Fresh lime leaves
- 2 Lemongrass sticks
- Half a bunch of coriander
- 1 tsp. ground cumin
- 1 tsp. ground coriander
- A couple of basil leaves (Thai if possible)

- 2 tbsp. Demerera sugar
- 2 tbsp. Fish sauce

Preparation – 45 to 50 minutes

1. Skin and roughly chop up the shallots.

2. Deseed the 2 red chilies.

3. Peel the garlic gloves.

4. Remove the outer skin from the lemongrass sticks and then finely slice them.

5. Wash the half bunch of coriander. Separate the leaves and stalks. (The leaves are for step 11, the stalks for step 6)

6. Put the chopped shallots, deseeded chilies, garlic gloves, coriander stalks, lemongrass, cumin, lime leaves into a food processor and blitz until you have a smooth curry paste.

7. Using a large pan over a medium heat add the olive oil and heat the oil until hot before adding the curry paste. Stir constantly whilst cooking the paste until the moisture has evaporated.

8. Now add in the 28 oz. (830ml) of coconut milk, gently bring to the boil. You can now add in some sugar and fish sauce to taste. Reduce the heat and maintain a gentle simmer for 10 minutes.

9. Whilst the sauce is simmering you can prepare the duck breasts. Remove the skin and then cut

up into 1 inch (2 cm) pieces. *Note: Now would be a good time to start cooking your rice if you have not already started.

10.   Add the cut up duck breast to the sauce and maintain the simmer for another 10 minutes.

11.   Plate up with rice on the side of the plate and then you can garnish with the basil leaves and fresh coriander leaves (which where left over from step 5).

Duck a l'orange

This is the famous English interpretation of the classic French roasted duck recipe. Serve with roast potatoes (basted with duck fat if you have any available) and green beans. Neither the potatoes nor green beans are included in this recipe so bare this in mind and prepare accordingly.

Ingredients for 2 good servings

- 1 Whole Duck 5 lbs. (2 Kg)

- 8 Oranges

- 1 and half cups duck or chicken stock

- 2 tbsp. Arrowroot (or tapioca or potato starch)

- Half cup of Sugar

- 1 tbsp. Peychaud Bitters or Angostura.

- Half cup Grand Marnier (or Cointreau)

Preparation – 2 hours 15 minutes

The Duck:

1.   Preheat the oven to 500°F (260°C).

2.   Make sure that the Duck is thoroughly cleaned, innards, wing tips and any excess fat should all be removed.

3.   Freshly squeeze 6 of the oranges. This should yield approximately 2 cups of orange juice. Save this for the sauce. Reserve the rinds.

4.   Chop up the rinds of the 6 oranges and put them inside the duck.

5.   Put the duck on a baking rack over a baking sheet with about half an inch of water.

6.   Place into the now hot oven and bake until the skin turns a golden brown and is lightly crispy. This will take approximately 30 minutes.

7.   Now reduce the oven temperature to 300°F (150°C) and continue to cook for one hour.

The Sauce:

8.   Zest the remaining 2 oranges.

9.   Using a medium size pan, combine the freshly squeezed orange juice, the zest and half cup of sugar over medium to high heat and reduce to approximately three quarters of a cup. Now you have the gastrique.

10.   Add the Peychaud Bitters to this gastrique and then set aside.

11.   You will now need to prepare, of have prepared your duck or chicken stock. A short cut here is to use duck or even chicken stock from a packet. Heat the stock up until it is hot.

12.   Now add two cups of stock to the gastrique and simmer over a medium heat for 8-10 minutes which so that it reduces.

13. Dissolve 2 tbsp. of arrowroot in 2 tbsp. of cold water. Add the arrowroot to the mixture to thicken. Note, if you cannot get arrowroot try potato or tapioca starch.

14. Remove the duck from the oven and take out of the roasting pan. You can throw away the fat from the pan if you like, but even better, save it to baste roast potatoes with another time.

15. Remove the orange rinds from inside the Duck and leave the duck stand for 10 minutes before carving it.

16. Now add the half cup of Grand Marnier (or Cointreau) to the now empty roasting pan and place over a medium high heat.

17. Using a wooden spoon deglaze the pan and reduce for 8 - 10 minutes.

18. The orange sauce from the pan can be served in a gravy boat along with the meal.

19. Serve the carved duck with roast potatoes and green beans and splash some of the orange sauce over the duck meat.

Peking Duck

When you think of Chinese duck recipes this is the classic recipe that comes to mind. A number of the other recipes in this book call for a Chinese roast duck. You can either buy one at your local Chinese supermarket or better cook one yourself using this recipe.

Serve this Peking duck with rice or potatoes and some vegetables. These are not included in this recipe so please take that into account.

Ingredients for 4 servings

- 1 Duck 5 lbs. (2 Kg) dressed

- 5 Scallions

- 3 tbsp. Soy sauce

- 1 Orange

- Half cup Plum jam

- Half tsp. Ground nutmeg

- Half tsp. Ground ginger

- Half tsp. Ground cinnamon

- Qtr. tsp. Ground white pepper

- 1/8 tsp. Ground cloves

- 1 tbsp. Honey

- 1 tbsp. fresh parsley

- 1 and Half tsp. sugar

- 1 and Half tsp. distilled white vinegar

- Qtr. cup finely chopped chutney

Preparation - 4 hours+

1. Thoroughly rinse the duck both inside and out. Then gently pat dry the duck.

2. If the tail is still attached, remove it and discard it.

3. Put the ground ginger, ground nutmeg, ground cinnamon, ground white pepper and ground cloves into a bowl and thoroughly mix together.

4. Sprinkle half of the spice mixture into the duck cavity.

5. Stir together the other half of the spice mixture with one tbsp. of the soy sauce. Rub this evenly over the body of the duck.

6. Cut in half one of the Scallions and place inside the duck cavity.

7. Cover the duck and refrigerate for at least 3 hours. If possible prepare the duck the day before you wish to cook and leave it overnight.

8. Using a large pot or wok place the duck so that it is breast side up and then steam the duck for

one hour. Note you may need to add more water as it evaporates so keep an eye it.

9. Remove the duck from the pot or wok and drain the juices and remove the scallion from inside the duck.

10. Preheat the oven to 380°F (195°C).

11. When the oven is at temperature place the duck on a roasting pan duck (breast side up) and using a fork prick the skin all over.

12. Roast the duck for half and hour.

13. Whilst the duck is roasting mix together the honey and the remaining 2 tbsp. of soy sauce.

14. After the half hour of roasting (from step 12) brush the honey mixture all over the duck and put the duck back in the oven.

15. Raise the oven temperature to 500°F (260°C) and roast for 5 to 10 minutes or until the skin has turned a rich brown color. Just make sure that the skin does not char.

16. To prepare the duck sauce: Mix the plum jam, chutney, vinegar and sugar together. Put in a small serving bowl.

17. Chop up the 4 remaining scallions and put them in bowl.

18. Slice the orange into rounds and chop up the parsley.

19. Put the duck onto a serving platter and garnish with the orange slices and fresh parsley.

20. Use the plum sauce and chopped scallion for dipping.

21. Carve the duck and serve with your choice of rice, potatoes and vegetables.

Peking Duck Pancakes

This traditional Chinese Peking duck pancakes make a great snack or can be used as part of a meal served with rice. These are simple, fun and tasty. No need to go to your local Chinese restaurant to enjoy these anymore.

Ingredients for 4 good servings

- 1 Peking duck – from a Chinese supermarket or use the Peking Duck Recipe in this book.
- Half cup Plain flour
- 6 Scallions
- 2 tbsp. Cornflour
- 2 Eggs
- Qtr. a cup of Water
- Qtr. a cup of Milk
- 2 tbsp. Butter
- Half a cup of Hoisin sauce

Preparation - 45 minutes

1. Melt the butter. This can be zapped in the microwave or even better using a small pan.

2. Crack the eggs and along with the flour, cornflour, milk, water and butter put into a food processor.

3. Process until the batter is smooth, then pour into a jug and cover and let stand for 15 minutes.

4. Gently brush a thin layer of butter into a non-stick frying pan and then place it over a medium heat.

5. Pour a tablespoonful of the batter into the frying pan and spread it out to form a thin pancake.

6. For each pancake cook on the first side for 2 minutes, then turn over and cook for another 1 minute on the other side.

7. Place each pancake on a plate and then repeat step 6 until you have used up all of the batter.

8. Ideally you will want to have the duck hot or warm. But first you can remove the skin and meat from the duck itself.

9. Thinly slice both the meat and the skin.

10. Cut the Scallions into lengths of 3 to 4 inches (8-12 cm).

11. In each pancake place some of the duck meat and skin together with a couple of Scallion lengths and tsp. of hoisin sauce.

12. Roll up and enjoy.

Duck Fried Rice with Celery Cabbage

Here is an example of a healthy yet tasty fried rice recipe. This is great to make if you have a bit of duck left over from the day before.

Ingredients for 4 servings

- 1 cup Cooked duck meat, cut in pieces

- 1 lb. (450 g) Long grain white rice

- 1 small head Celery cabbage

- 5 tbsp. Peanut oil

- 2 Shallots

- 2 Large eggs

- 2 Garlic cloves

- 2-inch (2 cm) piece of fresh ginger

- A pinch of red pepper flakes

- 8oz (225 g) can of Straw Mushrooms

- Half cup of Frozen peas

- A pinch sea salt

- 3 tbsp. of Soy sauce

- Fresh cilantro leaves, for garnish

Preparation – 45 to 50 minutes

1. Put the rice on to cook for 15 to 20 minutes. Use 2 parts water to 1 part rice. When the rice is cooked set it aside. Whilst the rice is cooking you can continue with steps 2 to 14.

2. Thinly slice the shallots after peeling the skins.

3. Mince the garlic cloves after peeling the skins.

4. Peel the skin from the ginger and then grate the ginger.

5. Core and chop the celery cabbage.

6. Run the frozen peas under cool water and leave then to thaw for a few minutes.

7. In a large non-stick frying pan or wok heat 3 tbsp. of the peanut over a medium to high heat.

8. When the oil is hot add the shallots, ginger, garlic, and red pepper flakes and stir-fry for approximately 1 minute until fragrant.

9. Add the cabbage, the mushrooms, and the peas, stir-fry until the cabbage is wilted and soft. This takes approximately 8 to10 minutes and then season with a pinch of salt.

10. Remove the vegetables from the wok and place to one side. Then wipe out the wok or frying pan with kitchen towel.

11. Place the wok or frying pan back over the medium to high heat and put 2 tbsp. of peanut oil into the wok/frying pan.

12. Whilst the oil is heating up lightly beat the 2

eggs.

13. When the oil is hot, add the lightly beaten eggs into the wok or frying pan, scramble it lightly. Let the egg set without stirring it too much so that it remains in large pieces.

14. By now the rice should be cooked. So fold it in with the egg to combine well.

15. Moisten the sauteed vegetables with the soy sauce and add to the wok or frying pan.

16. Mix everything together and heat through.

17. If the cooked meat is not hot you may want to put it in the microwave for a minute or two.

18. Put the fried rice onto a serving platter and place the warm duck pieces on top and then garnish with cilantro.

Sweet and Sour Duck with Noodles

No recipe book on ducks would be complete without a sweet and sour duck recipe. So here you have a tangy tasty recipe that will please all the family.

Ingredients for 4 good servings

- 4 Duck breasts - about 20 oz. (570 g)

- 1 lb. (450 g) packet of Noodles (Hokkien)

- 0.5 lb. (225 g) Pek Chye,

- 2 Red peppers

- 8 Spring onions

- 3 oz. (90 ml) Plum sauce

- 2 tbsp. Rice vinegar

- 2 tbsp. Soy sauce

- 2 tbsp. Tomato paste

- 2 tbsp. Vegetable oil

- 1 oz. (30 g) Fresh ginger

Preparation – 40 to 50 minutes

1. Deseed and thinly slice the red peppers lengthways.

2. Slice both the pek chye and spring onions lengthways.

3. Peel the fresh ginger and then cut it into strips.

4. Skin and thinly slice the duck breasts.

5. Mix together the tomato paste, plum sauce, soy sauce and vinegar in a bowl and set aside.

6. Place a wok or large non-stick frying pan over a high heat. Add the vegetable oil.

7. When the oil is hot stir-fry the spring onions and ginger for about 30 seconds.

8. Now add the duck slices and stir-fry for about 2 to 3 minutes. The duck should now be lightly cooked.

9. Next add the red peppers to the wok and stir-fry for a further 4 to 6 minutes. Both the duck and peppers should be tender.

10. Pour the sauce mixture (step 5) into the wok and toss everything together thoroughly and heat through.

11. Add the chopped pek chye to the wok and stir-fry for a further minute.

12. Boil some water to soak the noodles in. Soak them in hot water for 2 minutes and untangle them.

13.   Now put the noodles into the wok and stir-fry for 2 to 3 minutes, then serve.

Red Thai Duck Curry with Lychees

Another delicious Thai curry that your taste buds will love. This dish is best served with rice, which is not included as part of the recipe so please take not of this to prepare accordingly. Thai Jasmine rice goes very nicely with this dish.

Ingredients for 4 servings

- 3 Duck breasts

- 2 cups (450 ml) Coconut cream

- 12 fresh lychees

- 0.5 lb. (225 g) Cherry tomatoes

- Qtr. cup red curry paste

- 2 tbsp. Fish sauce

- 2 tbsp. Vegetable oil

- 1 tbsp. Brown sugar

- Half cup Thai basil leaves

- 6 Fresh lime leaves - kaffir if possible

- A Handful of Basil leaves

Preparation – 30 minutes

1. Preheat the oven to 390°F (200°C).

2. Line a baking tray with baking paper so that it is ready for the duck at step 6.

3. Using a non-stick frying pan heat the vegetable oil over medium to high heat.

4. When the oil is hot add duck breasts skin-side-down and cook for 2 minutes or until browned. Note you may have to do one breast at a time depending on gut size of your frying pan.

5. Then turn the duck breasts over in the pan and cook for 2 minutes.

6. When cooked put each duck breast on the baking try lined with the baking paper.

7. When all the duck breasts are cooked place the baking tray in the oven and roast for 8 minutes, then set aside.

8. In a deep pan heat half a cup of coconut cream over medium to high heat. Bring this to the boil and then add the curry paste and stir thoroughly.

9. Cook this for 2 minutes.

10. Diagonally slice the duck breasts.

11. Add the remaining cup of coconut cream together with the sliced duck breasts, fish sauce and sugar and duck.

12. Reduce the heat to medium and simmer for 5 minutes, which will allow the sauce to thicken.

13. Peel and deseed the lychees.

14. Add the lychees, cherry tomatoes, basil and lime leaves to the pan and cook for 2 minutes.

15. Serve the curry with rice on the side and enjoy.

Szechuan Pepper Duck

This is a very tasty recipe that will fill the house with a beautiful aroma whilst cooking.

* Steamed Jasmine Rice not included in this recipe - take note.

Ingredients for 4 servings

- 1 Duck 5 lbs. (2 kg)
- 2 inch (5 cm) Fresh ginger
- Qtr. cup (45g) whole blanched almonds
- 1 bunch baby Bok Choy, quartered lengthways
- 1 Bunch Choy sum, coarsely chopped
- 1 tsp. Chinese five spice
- 1 tbsp. sea salt
- 1 tsp. Szechuan pepper - ground
- 2 tbsp. Dry sherry
- 2 tbsp. Keycap manis (sweet soy sauce)
- 1 tbsp. Peanut oil
- 1 tbsp. Soy sauce
- Steamed jasmine rice, to serve

Preparation – 2 hours

1.   Preheat the oven to 390°F (200°C).

2.   Wash the duck inside and out and then pat it dry with a paper towel.

3.   Pierce all over the breast of the duck.

4.   Peel and thinly slice the ginger.

5.   Place the ginger in the duck cavity.

6.   Place the duck, breast-side down, in a large roasting pan.

7.   Combine the sherry, Chinese five spice and kecap manis in a bowl.

8.   Brush half of the sherry mixture over the duck.

9.   Place the duck uncovered in the now hot oven and roast for 30 minutes.

10.   Remove the duck from the oven and turn it breast side up.

11.   Reduce the oven temperature to 360°F (180°C).

12.   Brush the duck with the remaining sherry mixture and return to the oven and roast for 45 minutes.

13.   Remove the duck from oven and now turn it breast side down.

14.   Return the duck to the oven and roast for 30 minutes or until the juices run clear when the thigh is pierced with a skewer. * This is a good

time to start preparing/cooking the rice.

15. Turn the oven off and transfer the duck to a heatproof serving platter.

16. Loosely cover the duck with foil and return to the oven to keep warm.

17. Heat a small frying pan over low heat.

18. Add the szechuan pepper and sea salt and cook for 1 minute.

19. Remove the frying pan from the heat and set it aside.

20. Heat 1 tbsp. of oil in a wok over high heat until just smoking.

21. Add the almonds and stir-fry for 2 minutes so that they are toasted.

22. Transfer the almonds to a plate.

23. Heat 1 tbsp. of oil in the same wok over high heat until just smoking.

24. Quarter the bok choy lengthways and chop up the choy sum.

25. Add both the bok choy and choy sum to the wok and stir-fry for 3 minutes.

26. Add the toasted almonds and soy sauce to the wok and stir-fry for 1 minute.

27. Cut the duck along either side of the backbone. Remove and discard the backbone.

28. Cut the duck in half again to make 4 equal

portions.

29.   Put the rice into serving bowls and top with the almond mixture and pieces of duck.

30.   Sprinkle the duck with the szechuan pepper mixture and serve.

Duck Tagliatelle

This is an easy and quick dish to prepare and gives us an Italian style duck dish. This will please any pasta lovers out there and will be sure to please the children and parents alike.

Ingredients for 4 servings

- One large duck breast 7 oz. (200g)
- 1 lb. (450 g) of Tagliatelle egg pasta
- 1 lb. (450 g) of cooked tomato sauce (1 can)
- 7 oz. (200 ml) of Double cream
- 1 White onion
- 1 oz. (30 g) of dried Porchini mushroom
- 2 Garlic cloves
- Grated parmesan
- Black pepper
- Salt

Preparation – 30 minutes

1. Heat a frying pan and fry the duck breast fat side down then flip and fry on the other side.

2.   When the duck breast is cooked how you like (some like it rarer than others) remove it from the frying pan. Cut into quarter inch (0.5 cm) thick slices.

3.   Finely chop the garlic cloves and dice the onion.

4.   Add the chopped garlic cloves to the same frying pan and cook until brown and then remove them.

5.   Add the diced onion to the same frying pan and cook until soft.

6.   Add the sliced duck to the frying pan along with the porchini mushrooms and 1 - 2 oz (50 ml) of the water from the porchini mushrooms for added flavor.

7.   Cook for 3 to 4 minutes until the stock is reduced.

8.   Add the tomato sauce and cream to the same frying pan. Season to your taste with the salt and pepper.

9.   Turn the heat to low.

10. For the pasta, put a saucepan on the cooker with water and bring the water to the boil.

11. Add the tagliatelle to the saucepan with a tbsp.. of vegetable oil and two pinches of salt.

12. Stir the tagliatelle every few minutes so that they don't stick together.

13. When the tagliatelle is cooked, drain it, and then put in to the frying pan with the sauce or vice

versa depending on the size of pans that you have.

14. Give the tagliatelle and sauce a good stir.

15. Serve with some grated parmesan on top.

Roast Duck Fried Rice

This is a great recipe for using up leftovers from the Peking duck recipe in this book. Or, you can buy half of a roasted duck in a Chinese supermarket.

Note that rice is needed for this recipe so you can either use leftovers or prepare 2 cups of white rice.

Ingredients for 4 servings

- Half Roasted Duck - buy from a Chinese Market or use leftovers.
- 3 Carrots
- 2 Eggs
- 1 Bunch Scallions, sliced
- 1 tbsp. of Peanut oil
- Half a tsp. Soy sauce
- 2 cups White rice
- Qtr. tsp. Sesame oil

Preparation – 45 minutes

1. Bring at least 4 cups of water to boil in a saucepan.

2. Add the rice to the pan and cook. This rice will be needed in step 15.

3. Remove the duck meat and skin from the bones. Dice the duck meat into small pieces.

4. Preheat a large non-stick frying pan over a medium to high heat.

5. Combine the eggs with the soy sauce, the sesame oil, and a pinch of salt. Beat this thoroughly until completely mixed.

6. Add the diced duck meat to the now hot frying pan and cook through, stir constantly until the meat is crispy.

7. Remove duck meat from the frying pan and set aside.

8. Peel and dice the carrots.

9. Slice the bunch of scallion.

10. Add the peanut oil to the frying pan, followed by the carrots and scallions.

11. Cook constantly stirring for 3 to 4 minutes.

12. Remove the mixture from frying pan and set aside. The pan should still have a thin sheen of oil. If not, then add a bit more peanut oil before continuing.

13. Add the egg mixture to the frying pan and cook through for approximately one minute.

14. Remove the mixture from the frying pan. The pan should still have a thin sheen of oil. If not, then add a bit more peanut oil before

continuing.

15. Add the cooked rice to frying pan and stir-fry for 4 to 5 minutes until it is browning.

16. Return the duck, scallions, egg, and carrot to the frying pan and mix together with the rice for approximately 2 minutes.

17. Add the soy sauce to the pan and it is now ready to serve.

Roast Duck with Balsamic Vinegar and Honey Glaze

Here is a tasty European style recipe for roast duck. Note that no sides are included in the recipe. Roast potatoes and vegetables of your choice are recommended. Please plan for these when preparing this recipe.

Ingredients for 4 servings

- 1 Duck, 5 lbs. (2 Kg)
- 11 tbsp. Balsamic vinegar
- Qtr. cup Honey
- Half a tsp. Black pepper
- Half a tsp. Red Wine vinegar
- Salt and Pepper to season

Preparation - 1 hour 50 minutes

1. Preheat the oven to 425°F (220°C).

2. Remove the giblets from the duck and rinse the duck under cold water.

3. Season the duck cavity and skin generously with salt and pepper.

4.   Tie together the legs of the duck with string.

5.   Roast the duck, breast side up for 20 minutes.

6.   Remove the duck from the oven and rake the skin with a sharp fork. Be careful that you do not pierce the duck meat though.

7.   Return the duck to the oven and roast for a further 1 hour 15 minutes.

8.   Whilst the duck is roasting, baste it with the juices in the roasting pan.

9.   Also while duck is roasting, you can create the glaze. First combine the honey, 10 tbsp. of balsamic vinegar and half a tsp. of black pepper in small saucepan.

10.   Bring the mixture to the boil over a high heat.

11.   Boil the mixture until it starts to thicken.

12.   Stir the mixture constantly until it is thick and reduced to about 3 to 4 tablespoons.

13.   Remove the pan from the heat and add 1 tbsp. of balsamic vinegar along with the red wine vinegar.

14.   Keep the glaze mixture warm until the duck is cooked. Note. If the glaze cools and becomes thick then warm it over a low heat and stir.

15.   When the duck is cooked remove it from the oven and dry the skin with paper towels.

16.   Brush the duck with a thick coat of the warm glaze and put the duck back in the oven for 1 minute.

17.   Remove the duck from the oven and serve immediately with vegetables and potatoes or pasta.

Sticky Marmalade Duck Breast

This is a very easy recipe to cook and you can try this out if you don't feel like cooking duck a l'orange for example. Note that this dish goes great with either salad or steamed vegetables, neither of which are included so please take note and prepare accordingly.

Ingredients for 4 servings

- 4 Medium Duck Breasts

- 2 Oranges

- 8oz. (225 g) Orange Marmalade

- 4 tbsp. Soy Sauce

- Sea Salt

- Salad or steamed Vegetables to serve

Preparation - 45 minutes

1. Preheat the oven to 380°F (195°C)

2. Score the skin of the duck breast with a sharp knife and create a criss-cross pattern.

3. Sprinkle a little sea salt on the skin.

4. Heat a frying pan over a medium to high heat.

5. Skin side down cook the duck breast for 4

minutes or until the skin is a golden brown.

6.   Turn the duck breast over and cook for 2 minutes.

7.   Depending on the size of your frying pan you may have to repeat steps 5 and 6 numerous times. If so keep the cooked duck breasts covered while you finish cooking the others.

8.   Combine the soy sauce and orange marmalade and use this to coat the duck breasts.

9.   Using a large pan roast the duck breasts in the oven for 8 to 10 minutes. Note, baste the duck every couple of minutes.

10.   Remove the duck breasts from the oven and transfer them from the pan and place them on a warm plate to rest.

11.   Zest and segment the 2 oranges.

12.   Add the orange zest and segments to the pan used to roast the duck and place into the oven.

13.   Let the orange simmer for several minutes until the sauce is sticky and has reduced, then remove from the oven.

14.   Thinly slice the duck breast and place it onto serving plates.

15.   Drizzle the sticky sauce over the thinly sliced duck breast.

16.   Serve with either steamed vegetables or salad.

Pan Fried Duck Breast with Braised Lentils

This is another healthy yet delicious duck recipe. The contrast between the lentils and the rich moist duck makes for a real treat.

Ingredients for 4 servings

- 4 Duck breasts

- 10 oz. (280 g) Green (puy) lentils

- 4 Portobello mushrooms

- 1 Red onion

- 2 tbsp. Sherry vinegar

- 2 tbsp. Olive oil

- 2 tbsp. Walnut oil

- Half a cup of parsley

- Salt and pepper

Preparation - 1 hour

1. Rinse the lentils with cold water and place them in a saucepan.

2. Add enough water to the saucepan to completely cover the lentils and then bring them to the boil over a medium heat.

3. When the water is boiling reduce the heat and leave to simmer for 20 to 25 minutes. Note that you may need to add a little water during this step so keep an eye on the saucepan.

4. Now that the lentils are cooked you can drain them and set them aside. Ideally you want the lentils to still have a little bit of a bite to them.

5. Mix together 1 tbsp. of the walnut oil and 1 tbsp. of the sherry vinegar.

6. Drizzle the mixture over the still warm lentils. Also add a couple of pinches of salt and pepper to season.

7. Using a sharp knife make a criss-cross pattern in the duck skin of each breast. Cut through to the duck meat but do not cut the meat itself.

8. Season the duck breasts on both sides with salt and pepper.

9. Place a large non-stick frying pan or skillet over a medium to high heat.

10. Skin side down place the duck breasts in the frying pan. Cook for 8 minutes and the then turn the duck breasts over and cook for 4 minutes.

11. The duck breast should now be a little pink on the inside. Adjust the cooking times depending on your taste. Note that you may have to make

two batches for the duck breasts depending on the size of your pan. If so, slightly undercook the first duck breasts and leave them to rest under foil, they will continue to cook for a couple of minutes when you take them off the heat.

12. Make sure that all the cooked duck breasts have been left to rest for at least 5 minutes underneath foil. Do not clean out the frying pan because it is needed in step 15.

13. Cut the red onion in half and then thinly slice it.

14. Rinse and then thickly slice the 4 portobello mushrooms.

15. Without having cleaned the frying pan place it back on the medium to high heat and add the onions and cook until they soft.

16. Add the sliced mushrooms to the pan and cook for 5 minutes. Stir whilst cooking.

17. Remove the frying pan from the heat and then fold the onions and mushrooms into the still warm lentils.

18. Serve the lentils on 4 plates, and then top with the duck breasts.

19. Drizzle 1 tbsp. of walnut oil, 1 tbsp. of olive oil and 1 tbsp. of sherry vinegar over the duck breasts.

20. Freshly chop the half cup of parsley and sprinkle on top of each plate and serve.

Duck Cassoulet

No duck recipe book should miss out this French classic. This is a truly awesome dish that although it takes a bit of work is worth every second spent in preparing it.

Ingredients for 4 servings

- 4 Confit Duck legs

- 20 oz. (670 g) Dried haricot beans

- 10 oz. (280 g) Garlic sausages

- 5 oz. (140 g) Pork rind

- 5 oz. (140 g) Smoked bacon or lardons

- 2 oz. (55 g) Dried breadcrumbs

- 7 Garlic cloves

- 1 Bouquet garni

- 1 Onion

- 1 Celery stick

- 1 Carrot

- 1 Clove

- 4 tbsp. Olive oil

- 2 tsp. Lemon juice

- 1 handful of fresh parsley

- Salt and Pepper

Preparation - 5 hours+ Overnight soak

1. The night before you wish to prepare this dish soak the 20 oz. of dried haricot beans in 3 times their volume of water. You will want these to soak for at least 10 hours.

2. Roll up the pork rind as if it was a Swiss roll. Make sure the seam is underneath and then cut the roll (across) into thin slices with a sharp knife. Next dice the rolled up slices by cutting them across.

3. In you bought lardons instead of bacon proceed to step 4. If not, the chop the bacon into small cubes that resemble lardons.

4. Cut the sausage up into half inch (1 cm) thick slices.

5. Drain the haricot beans that have been soaking from the night before.

6. In a large saucepan put the drained haricot beans, the diced bacon (or lardons), the diced pork rind and cover with water.

7. Bring the saucepan to the boil and blanch for 20 minutes.

8. Drain the contents of the saucepan ensuring that all the cooking water is discarded.

9. Roughly chop up the carrot, celery and onion.

10. Peel the skin from 6 garlic cloves leaving them whole.

11. Preheat the oven to 250°F (120°C).

12. Put 2 tbsp. of olive oil in a large deep ovenproof casserole dish and place over a low heat.

13. Peel and roughly chop up both the carrot and the onion.

14. Wash and roughly chop up the celery stick.

15. Add the carrot, celery, garlic and onion to the casserole dish and sweat for 5 minutes.

16. Add the bouquet garni to the casserole dish and continue to cook for another 5 minutes.

17. Add the beans, diced bacon (lardons), sausage, the pork rind and 2 pints of water to the casserole dish.

18. Bring the casserole dish to the boil. Then remove any scum from the surface. Season with salt and pepper and add the lemon juice and the clove (lightly crush it before adding).

19. Put the uncovered casserole dish in the oven and cook for 2 hours 15 minutes. Give it a good stir after the first hour.

20. Peel and finely chop the remaining garlic clove.

21. When the beans are soft and the juice has thickened you can remove the casserole dish from the oven.

22. Submerge the duck legs underneath the beans.

23. Add the breadcrumbs, the finely chopped garlic clove and cover with 2 tbsp. of olive oil.

24. Place the casserole dish back in the oven for 2

hours.

25.   Finely chop the parsley.

26.   Remove the casserole from the oven and serve in bowls, sprinkling the parsley on top of each.

8595945R00050

Printed in Great Britain
by Amazon.co.uk, Ltd.,
Marston Gate.